STUDY GUIDE

BUILDING A

KILLER
TEAM

Published by Inspire and AVAIL

For foreign and subsidiary rights, contact the author

Cover design by: Bogdan Matei

ISBN: 978-1-957369-14-3   1 2 3 4 5 6 7 8 9 10

Printed in the United States of America

STUDY GUIDE

BUILDING A

KILLER TEAM

WITHOUT KILLING
YOURSELF OR YOUR TEAM

SHAWN LOVEJOY

CONTENTS

MY CONFESSIONS (AND YOURS)

The most encouraging news of this book is that leadership can be learned. I got better, I improved, and I learned. I hired coaches and sought perspective. I read, I worked at it, I prayed about it, I journaled, I practiced, and I grew. I made progress and began to experience the fruits of my labor as I built a killer team.

Read Chapter 1: "My Confessions (and Yours)," in *Building A Killer Team Without Killing Yourself or Your Team,* reflect on the questions and discuss your answers with your study group.

Have you ever done "the right thing in the wrong way" and faced repercussions for doing so? How did that affect your leadership equity?

_____

_____

_____

_____

What does Shawn mean when he says we should build people, not things?

_____

_____

_____

_____

Have you ever been a part of a killer team? What did that team exhibit that made them "killer"?

_____

_____

_____

_____

What sort of setback do you think a leader would encounter as they attempt to build a killer team?

_____

_____

_____

_____

chapter 2

THE DISTINCTIONS AND PILLARS OF A KILLER TEAM

I can say with absolute confidence that I can trace every tension and opportunity in your organization back to one of three areas: the culture, the team, or the systems.

What is the difference between a staff and a team?

_____

_____

_____

_____

_____

Why should a leader slow down and explain the details? How is this better than flying solo?

_____

_____

_____

_____

_____

_____

_____

_____

Share some real-world examples of sending problems up and praise down.

_____

_____

_____

_____

_____

_____

How does a leader encourage honesty among team members?

_____

_____

_____

_____

_____

_____

Why is consistency better than perfection?

_____

_____

_____

_____

How do praise, honesty, and consistency lead to healthy teams: practicing good habits, clear communication, and defining realistic expectations?

_____

_____

_____

_____

_____

_____

_____

_____

_____

_____

What specific tensions keep you awake at night?

_____

_____

_____

_____

_____

_____

chapter 3

FOSTERING TOGETHERNESS

You must get clearer about your expectations. You must get clearer about the vision. You've got to get clearer about your strategy. You have to clear away the clutter. People today are looking for meaningful and fulfilling work, and you've got to provide it. It's not just what you're doing; it's why you do it.

Why do you think Shawn suggests you go beyond wanting togetherness to *fostering* togetherness? What is the difference?

_____

_____

_____

_____

_____

_____

Consider the milk scenario. What are some ways in which you have been unclear with team members?

_____

_____

_____

_____

_____

How can you trace a "people tension" back to a "system tension"?

_____

_____

_____

_____

_____

_____

n what ways can you help people "feel like they are experiencing real growth and development under your leadership"?

_____

_____

_____

_____

Are you currently meeting with your direct reports weekly? What do you think the benefits of doing so would be?

_____

_____

_____

_____

Consider the statement: "One of my roles as a leader is to help each person discover and embrace the value of sharing life, doing life together, and discovering the strength we have together." How do you see yourself filling this role?

_____

_____

_____

_____

What good things happen in a meeting? Why should you focus on those things?

_____

_____

_____

_____

_____

What are the three components of the team that helped establish
Christianity?

_____

_____

_____

_____

_____

_____

How can people be simultaneously devoted to the mission and to
each other?

_____

_____

_____

_____

_____

_____

What is the best way to get your team members to think how you
think?

_____

_____

_____

_____

_____

chapter 4

THE FIVE PURPOSES OF MEETINGS

*Leaders won't buy in unless they weigh in. So,
I'm always also looking for opportunities to
tackle strategic issues with my team. Instead
of feeling like I have to solve them on my own,
I invite my team to be part of the process.*

Describe how you can have meetings that matter. What does that mean in your organization?

_____

_____

_____

_____

_____

_____

_____

_____

_____

_____

How does holding consistent meetings prevent silos from forming?

_____

_____

_____

_____

_____

_____

_____

_____

_____

_____

Consider Shawn's statement that we meet because we care. In what ways do you agree or disagree? How does meeting show you care?

_____

_____

_____

_____

_____

Why is it important for team members to know what others are working on?

_____

_____

_____

_____

How can your team benefit from a "just so you know" style of interaction?

_____

_____

_____

_____

Why is inviting feedback from team members critical to the success of your vision?

_____

_____

_____

_____

How can you use coaching conversations to tackle issues? Why should you do this when issues are minimal?

_____

_____

_____

_____

_____

_____

What are the dangers of becoming a "politician encourager"? What are some specific ways that you can encourage team members today?

_____

_____

_____

_____

How would you rate yourself on these meeting components: community, communication, collaboration, coaching, and cheering? Which areas do you think you could use some help in?

_____

_____

_____

_____

_____

_____

_____

_____

chapter 5

NAILING YOUR VALUES AND BUILDING TRUST

If vision is the why and strategy is the what, values are the how. They determine how we behave while we do what it is we do.

Reading Time

Read Chapter 5: "Nailing Your Values and Building Trust," in *Building A Killer Team Without Killing Yourself or Your Team*, reflect on the questions and discuss your answers with your study group.

How does providing clarity for your team give a competitive advantage?

_____

_____

_____

_____

_____

_____

_____

What are your current core values? What are your team's? How do they compare?

_____

_____

_____

_____

_____

_____

How can a value be measurable and coach-able? What is the importance of values being so?

_____

_____

_____

_____

_____

_____

_____

Share some ways that you can build trust with your team members. How can they earn trust from you?

_____

_____

_____

_____

_____

_____

_____

Describe a time in which you had to say, "I'm sorry." How did that help rebuild trust on your team?

_____

_____

_____

_____

_____

_____

_____

What does Shawn mean by the "last ten percent"? Why is it such a big deal to push for team members to go "there"?

_____

_____

_____

_____

_____

How do you show grace to those on your team?

_____

_____

_____

_____

_____

How can you encourage your team to give you their gut-level honest feedback and answers?

_____

_____

_____

_____

_____

Which members of your team may need to be placed in an area that matches their skill set? How can you facilitate their success?

_____

_____

_____

_____

_____

RECRUITING (AND KEEPING) YOUR BEST TALENT

Many people will come and go over the years. Most people will not stay on your team for the long haul. Your goal is not to hang on to every team member forever, but to hold them loosely. They don't belong to you; they belong to God. He simply entrusts them to your care for a season. You want to be a good steward (manager) that wisely manages God's prized assets: people.

Read Chapter 6: "Recruiting (and Keeping) Your Best Talent," in *Building A Killer Team Without Killing Yourself or Your Team*, reflect on the questions and discuss your answers with your study group.

Why does killer talent *need* to be recruited?

_____

_____

_____

_____

_____

_____

_____

Name some compelling reasons why a person with killer talent should join your team.

_____

_____

_____

_____

_____

_____

Do you have the margin to look around inside your organization for rising stars? Whom can you recruit from within?

_____

_____

_____

_____

_____

_____

What is the danger of only hiring "technicians" to fill roles on your team? Share a time when that has backfired on you.

_____

_____

_____

_____

_____

_____

What are the four filters for choosing and retaining team members?

_____

_____

_____

_____

_____

_____

What is the primary reason that new hires fail in their role with a team?

_____

_____

_____

_____

How can you recognize when a person has hit their capacity lid? What are your options once they do?

_____

_____

_____

_____

_____

Why is it better to "get divorced" before you "get married?"

_____

_____

_____

_____

Have you ever been guilty of overemphasizing one of the Cs? Which one and how did you reestablish balance for yourself and your team?

_____

_____

_____

_____

_____

_____

DEVELOPING YOUR TEAM

Your job as a leader is to love your team members enough to refuse to allow them to get too comfortable. You want to squeeze every ounce of potential out of them. . . . . In today's world, people are quitting jobs that pay more and are accepting less to be in a growth environment.

Read Chapter 7: "Developing Your Team," in *Building A Killer Team Without Killing Yourself or Your Team,* reflect on the questions and discuss your answers with your study group.

Do you have a Team 411 list? If not, when do you plan to initiate this list creation?

_____

_____

_____

_____

_____

_____

_____

What does it mean to "systematize care"?

_____

_____

_____

_____

How have you been sharing content with your team? What are some resources that you can share with them over the coming weeks and months?

_____

_____

_____

_____

_____

_____

_____

What is the value of having a coach no matter how elite your status?

_____

_____

_____

_____

_____

In what ways can you nurture a coaching atmosphere for your team members?

_____

_____

_____

_____

_____

What does it mean to "fly at the next level"? How can you act like you belong?

_____

_____

_____

_____

Consider the six characteristics of a first-class leader. Rate yourself on them. What areas do you feel are first-class? What areas need a bump?

_____

_____

_____

_____

_____

_____

_____

_____

_____

_____

What are the three reasons that people leave teams?

_____

_____

_____

_____

_____

_____

How do those reasons resonate with your experience?

_____

_____

_____

_____

_____

_____

BOLSTERING ACCOUNTABILITY

It's time to bolster accountability on your team. I know, I know. You want to hold your team more accountable. It's easy to think about what our team members owe us and what we want to hold them accountable for, but what exactly are we accountable for to our team?

Reading Time

Read Chapter 8: "Bolstering Accountability," in *Building A Killer Team Without Killing Yourself or Your Team,* reflect on the questions and discuss your answers with your study group.

Why is the number one responsibility of a leader to *be* the culture you want to build?

_____

_____

_____

_____

_____

_____

_____

_____

_____

_____

_____

How do you set the example for culture in your organization?

_____

_____

_____

_____

_____

_____

_____

_____

_____

_____

_____

_____

What does this statement mean for you as a leader? "Culture happens by default or by design."

_____

_____

_____

_____

_____

_____

How do you inspire your team to be action-oriented?

_____

_____

_____

_____

_____

_____

_____

Are your team meetings action-oriented? How can you incorporate Shawn's template into your organization to increase accountability?

_____

_____

_____

_____

_____

_____

_____

REVIEWING YOUR TEAM

I let my team members know before the review that I am going to encourage, but I am also going to be a little hard on them. My job is to care about them enough to not allow them to stay the way they are. They have potential and growth inside of them that they don't even understand, and I want to call it out.

Read Chapter 9: "Reviewing Your Team," in *Building A Killer Team Without Killing Yourself or Your Team,* reflect on the questions and discuss your answers with your study group.

How is the team member review process that Shawn describes different from a staff evaluation?

_____

_____

_____

_____

_____

_____

_____

_____

_____

_____

Why do you think that high-level leaders "grade" themselves harshly?

_____

_____

_____

_____

_____

_____

_____

_____

_____

_____

Why is it important to define each category that a score falls under?

_____

_____

_____

_____

How similar to Shawn's review process is your current review system? Where are there areas of congruence?

_____

_____

_____

_____

_____

_____

What can you incorporate from Shawn's example into your organization's review process?

_____

_____

_____

_____

Why is the first component in a healthy performance and review process vision, clarity, and alignment?

_____

_____

_____

_____

_____

How can you utilize the review process as part of your hiring process?

_____

_____

_____

_____

_____

_____

_____

_____

RELEASING SOMEONE THE RIGHT WAY

You need to move them off the team, but how do you do it? Well, the right timing, tone, and temperature are all important. Often in leadership, coming to the conclusion of what needs to be done is only 25 percent of the process. Understanding how to do the right thing the right way is a full 75 percent of the process.

Reading Time

Read Chapter 10: "Releasing Someone the Right Way," in *Building A Killer Team Without Killing Yourself or Your Team,* reflect on the questions and discuss your answers with your study group.

Share a time when you allowed an unhealthy team member to remain on the team. What were the consequences of that?

_____
_____
_____
_____
_____
_____
_____
_____
_____
_____
_____

How does allowing underperforming people to remain on the team hurt your credibility as the leader?

_____
_____
_____
_____
_____
_____
_____
_____
_____

Why is *now* the best time to release someone?

_____

_____

_____

_____

_____

Why is it important to maintain dignity for the person you are releasing?

_____

_____

_____

_____

_____

_____

_____

What value do you see in sharing the pain you experienced in reaching that conclusion with the outgoing team member?

_____

_____

_____

_____

_____

_____

_____

_____

_____

Why should the exit agreement contain a cascading communication plan? What has been your experience without one?

_____

_____

_____

_____

_____

_____

_____

_____

_____

_____

STRUCTURING FOR GROWTH . . . AND PEACE

To build the killer team you need to build, you will need to pay more attention to your most precious commodity: your time. . . . Time is a more precious commodity than money, but we incessantly measure how much money we have in the bank and we manage how we spend it, but very few of us monitor as closely how we manage our time.

Read Chapter 11: "Structuring for Growth . . . and Peace," in *Building A Killer Team Without Killing Yourself or Your Team*, reflect on the questions and discuss your answers with your study group.

How do you feel that you do with managing your time?

_____

_____

_____

_____

_____

_____

_____

_____

What would you consider to be in your Fab 5 list?

_____

_____

_____

_____

_____

_____

How much time do you spend alone, working on yourself and the organization? If it's not 20 percent, how can you raise that percentage of time?

_____

_____

_____

_____

_____

_____

Consider the pizza rule. How does your structure fit into that model?

_____

_____

_____

_____

_____

_____

What is the danger of having two bosses? What trouble do you face relinquishing control to your team leads?

_____

_____

_____

_____

_____

_____

_____

What are the pitfalls of the CEO being the only product?

_____

_____

_____

_____

_____

_____

TENDENCIES THAT SABOTAGE OUR TEAM-BUILDING

The most difficult person you will ever lead is yourself. If you get better, everyone and everything else will get better too. So, leader, you must work on you.

How does a dull ax cause you to work "harder not smarter"?

_____

_____

_____

_____

_____

_____

_____

What warning signs in your own life let you know you need to sharpen your ax?

_____

_____

_____

_____

_____

_____

What are some specific ways that you can sharpen your ax?

_____

_____

_____

_____

_____

_____

_____

Have you ever found yourself occupied with working *in* the business and not *on* the business? What was the result?

_____

_____

_____

_____

_____

_____

Briefly describe your plan to grow yourself.

_____

_____

_____

_____

_____

_____

_____

How can a leader identify if they are life-sucking or life-giving?

_____

_____

_____

_____

_____

_____

_____

Have you ever succumbed to the lie that things will slow down? How long did it take you to realize that it wasn't going to happen?

_____

_____

_____

_____

_____

_____

_____

_____

chapter 13

INSPIRING YOUR TEAM

One of the best things you can do to retain your great leaders is have some fun together. They love seeing you in that environment. Be more spontaneous. Watch the energy return to the team.

Reading Time

Read Chapter 13: "Inspiring Your Team," in *Building A Killer Team Without Killing Yourself or Your Team,* reflect on the questions and discuss your answers with your study group.

Why do you think teams need cheerleaders when they are tired and bruised?

_____
_____
_____
_____
_____
_____
_____
_____
_____
_____

How can a vision leak like a balloon?

_____
_____
_____
_____
_____
_____
_____
_____
_____
_____

Why is it so important to know (and share) your *why*?

_____

_____

_____

_____

_____

_____

_____

What are some ways that you can consistently remind yourself of your *why*?

_____

_____

_____

_____

_____

_____

Are you a thermometer or a thermostat? How does that show up in your team?

_____

_____

_____

_____

_____

_____

_____

_____

_____

Who are the life-givers that speak into your life?

_____

_____

_____

_____

_____

_____

chapter 14

MAINTAINING RHYTHM AND FINISH LINES

If you want to build a killer team without killing yourself or your team, the number one thing I want for you at the end of all of this is to be able to finish well as a leader. Stay sane, centered, and married while you're building whatever it is you're building.

Read Chapter 14: "Maintaining Rhythm and Finish Lines," in *Building A Killer Team Without Killing Yourself or Your Team*, reflect on the questions and discuss your answers with your study group.

Why is it that leaders succeed or crumble from the inside out?

_____

_____

_____

_____

_____

_____

_____

_____

_____

_____

_____

Why is your health as a leader primary in determining your team's health?

_____

_____

_____

_____

_____

_____

_____

_____

_____

_____

_____

Why is it impossible to give equal time and energy to all things?

_____

_____

_____

_____

_____

_____

_____

What does it mean to pursue a life of rhythm?

_____

_____

_____

_____

_____

_____

How is it that our success is so closely correlated with living a life of rhythm?

_____

_____

_____

_____

_____

_____

Who do you consider to be an "upstream relationship"?

_____

_____

_____

_____

_____

_____

_____

_____

CPSIA information can be obtained
at www.ICGtesting.com
Printed in the USA
LVHW032243100522
718054LV00005B/24